TICKLEBELLY HILL

Grandparents Raising Grandchildren

by

Hilda Osborne

ISBN: 1-4033-9076-2 (e-book)
ISBN: 1-4033-9077-0 (Paperback)

This book is printed on acid free paper.

1stBooks – rev. 11/29/02

Prologue

"The journey is everything."

It has been said that getting there is half the fun. Any journey involves more than simply arriving at the hoped-for destination. Adventure and discovery are waiting at every turn, down every yet-to-be explored trail, and in places we were not expecting to find ourselves. No matter where our travels take us, whether it is down the street to what we think is familiar territory or around the world to some exotic location, wonders are waiting to reveal themselves to us. This truth applies not only to road trips but our journey through life as well. The journey from here to there is where plans are made, hopes are realized, and lessons are learned. The journey is also where some of life's most difficult situations are encountered and overcome, and where dreams are made, broken, and recreated.

The road from childhood to adulthood is covered with potholes, bumps, dead ends, and unexpected detours. Guiding children down that road is not an easy task, even for young parents. It is especially difficult for those of us making the journey a second time when with every push of our bodies all the long years of our lives push back. Simple tasks take twice the energy, and the desire to extend beyond only the necessary has diminished. But because we have been down that road before, we have learned which potholes to avoid, as well as which detours are worth taking. More importantly, we know that road should not be traveled too hastily. It is alright to stop and smell the roses, or watch a butterfly as it floats away on the wind, or stand in amazement as colorful leaves flutter down from trees that surely were planted by giants. We know to take the time while the time is there to look up in wonder at the stars, or to watch with awe the ocean waves as they move in and out against the shore. Years from now, and, yes, there will be more years of life at the end of raising grandchildren, we will remember the smiles, the laughter, the lessons taught, the lessons learned, and how our hearts excited at the re-discovery of long-held knowledge.

If I could wave a magic wand and the children I am raising today could become fully-grown, fully independent adults before bedtime tonight, I would break that wand and throw it out with yesterday's candy wrappers. I would not want to miss one step of this journey. I would not forfeit all those little treasures that are created in secret rooms with bits of crayon, colored paper and paste that come to be hung majestically from magnets on the refrigerator door. I would not give up being chosen to witness those proud Olympian moments that are preceded with "Watch what I can do!" But most of all, I would not want to wave away those unexpected moments when a child offers her arms in a hug just to say, "I love you, Granny," and I can wrap my arms around a bit of precious future and promises of grand tomorrows.

CHAPTER ONE

Introduction

A few years ago I would have thrown out this old thing. I paid less than ten dollars for it at the church's second-hand clothing store, and I had already gotten my money's worth out of it.

"But, Granny, it's my favorite," she had pleaded with me to sew up the rips in the lining of the old comforter. It was made for a single bed, but she liked to curl up under it and wrap herself in it on her full-sized bed. It was not all that colorful, printed in shades of gray and tan, but she liked the pictures of kittens strewn across it. They reminded her of the cats she had at her mother's house. That made it her favorite.

I hated sewing; I had given it up years ago. I never really had the patience for it, and my aging eyes make it harder and harder to see the needle, much less the nearly invisible thread that has to be pushed through that tiny hole at one end. How she had managed to make so many rips and tears in the lining, I will never know. But it was her favorite, and she wanted me to sew it up for her. So with the aid of a needle threader and bifocals, I manage to piece together the ripped places. It is not a pretty job, and there are still some frayed edges. But my 12-year-old granddaughter is thrilled with her "like new" comforter.

Cindy and her two sisters came to live with us when she was ten years old. Lesley was eight, and Summer was six. They are the daughters of my daughter. Each of the girls has a different father, and thus a different last name. Cindy and Summer have blonde hair, like their mother. Lesley is half African-American, like her father. They came to live with us after I fought for and won custody in court after state officials had taken them away from their mother. They were taken into protective custody because of abuse they were suffering at the hands of their mother's newest love interest, her third husband and umpteenth bad relationship. To leave them in foster care, even for what I would have hoped would be a short time, was simply unthinkable. To think of them living with strangers, separated from their family, broke my heart. They belonged with their family, and that meant they belonged with me.

Since the girls came to live with us almost four years ago, my daughter has made some improvements in her life, but is still not improved to a point where she can take care of her three little girls. Why she can't really is not an issue at this point. She simply can't. And since she can't, we must. Children are not something you can set aside until you are ready to raise them. They are an immediate-need situation. They need everything, and they need it immediately! So my husband Ben and I took on the task of raising these three little girls. Even as we accepted what the court called temporary custody, we knew there would be nothing temporary about it.

Ben and I had reached a point in our lives where we were comfortable. We are not wealthy, but money was not a problem. We owned two vehicles, a fishing boat for him, and a pontoon boat that we enjoyed sharing with family and friends. We had just built a house on an eleven-acre piece of land overlooking the lake. We enjoyed just being at home, strolling our little piece of land, and making plans for our future. We enjoyed a hobby of raising and showing German Shepherd Dogs. A work injury had disabled Ben a few years before, and taking care of the dogs gave him something to do with his days. We could load up the van on any weekend and head for a nearby dog show. Or, if we just wanted someplace to go for a couple of days, we could choose the mountains for the weekend. Decisions about dinner many times were not *what* we were going to eat, but *where* we were going to eat. Life was unstructured. I went to work and he planned his day around my hours. I work in a call center that is open 24 hours a day, and many times I would not get home till late at night. That was alright, though, because he could wait up for me, then we could both sleep late the next day. While I was working, he would clean house a little, as much as his disability would allow. He would plan and cook our meals, or we would meet somewhere for dinner, or I would bring home something from a nearby drive-through. I saw the grandchildren once or twice a month when

I would make the 150-mile drive to Nashville. Sometimes I would bring them home with me for a short visit. We played the role of typical grandparents, enjoying the children, pampering them, and treating them like the special children they are in our hearts. I loved having them with us, but I also loved taking them home again.

Now, however, we are their home. We have accepted the fact that the girls will be with us until they reach adulthood. It has been a major adjustment, and is not something I would have wished for, but I thank God that we are able to provide a secure home for them. If my daughter were to try to regain custody, I would not stand in her way, but losing the girls now after all this time would certainly leave an emptiness in our lives. My husband and I would have to readjust to life without a houseful of activity, and we would have to learn to be "just us" again.

We have adjusted our lives to fit in the activities of three busy little girls. We now keep scheduled hours to match school bus pickup and deliveries. We drop them off at skating rinks and friends' houses, and we accommodate their friends who come here to spend the night. We talk of birds and bees, and butterflies. We explore the world around us, and, when they initiate it, we discuss why bad men "do those things" to little girls. We have bonded more deeply than would have been possible if they had not come to live with us. They have become our children, and although we have had to give up many of the comforts we thought we would be enjoying at this stage of our life, no sacrifice is too great for providing a safe, secure and happy place for our grandchildren to grow.

Not long after the girls moved in with us, we realized we needed to make some cuts in our budget. We decided that our pontoon boat was a luxury we could live without.

After selling it, some friends noticed its absence and asked us about it.

My explanation would bring a laugh, "It was either sell the boat or sell one of the kids. I figured we would get more money for the boat!"

Hilda Osborne

CHAPTER TWO

Expectations

This is not what I had hoped for in the second half of my life. Three children can fill up a house, and a houseful of children at my age can be daunting. They want to go roller-skating; I want to curl up in my comfortable chair. They want to have friends over; I want to pull the curtains and draw the shades. They want to stay up late; I want to go to bed early. They hope for a bright future; I hope for quiet at the end of the day.

"Granny, will you play a game with me?" asks one of the girls.

I have been working all day, and I am tired. We have just finished dinner, and the dishes are barely cleared away. All homework questions, hopefully, have been answered and recorded on the appropriate worksheet or notebook. A load of clean clothes is tumbling in the dryer. When they are dry, I will have to take them out and hang up those items I do not want to become hopelessly wrinkled. Ironing is just one more chore I try to avoid. Tomorrow will be another day of getting up early enough to get the three girls dressed and ready to catch the school bus before 7:00am. My aging eyes want to close and my tired body wants to recline on anything soft. I have only enough energy left to sit and absently watch my favorite TV program. "Not right now, maybe tomorrow."

"Oh, okay," Her shoulders slump and her expression falls.

"Well, maybe just one game," I give in.

"Oh, okay!" Her expression brightens and she tells me how much fun this is going to be as she opens a board game or starts dealing out cards for a lively game of Go Fish.

Countless thousands of grandparents are raising their grandchildren. Circumstances vary from family to family that make raising the grandchildren a necessity. Some grandparents have assumed the task from their children, parents who started having children when they themselves were far too young to manage the tasks of parenthood, or had no means of supporting or nurturing their own children. Some grandparents have legal custody mandated by court order. Others have simply taken over the task of raising the children who are unwanted or neglected by their own adult children. Many more nurture from a distance those children whose legal address is with one or both of their natural parents but who are more at home in their grandparents' house. For some, it is a temporary situation; for so many others, it is a challenge that does not end until the children become adults and move out on their own.

Many parents watch helplessly as their adult children continue to have children they cannot or will not care for properly. They know the day will come when they will have to take over and become the parent if they do not want to see their grandchild go the way of so many unwanted or neglected children. Many more are taken by complete surprise when their seemingly healthy and intelligent children simple fail to properly care for their own children. Grandparents take over when their children fail their children, failing to guide, teach, nurture, or protect the innocent lives they so haphazardly brought into the world. Many grandparents blame themselves, wondering where they went wrong as parents. How could I have raised a child who cannot or will not care for his or her own children, they will ask themselves. In spite of being told it is not their fault, that children grow into adults who make their own decisions, and even children who were raised in good homes grow into people who make bad choices, many parents will still carry the weight of "what should I have done differently."

Several years ago my husband's job took us about 150 miles away from where my grandchildren would be born and raised. I tried to be as involved as I could from such a distance. I made the two-hour drive once or twice a month, always with the nagging knowledge that my daughter was in need of something. Whether it was money to pay her rent or diapers for the baby, she was always short of something. As one child became two, then two became three, and there was still no reliable mate in her life, my offers of help fell on deaf ears. My daughter only became resentful of any advise I tried to give. She always had an excuse, a defense for the way she lived her life. Jobs were hard to find and even harder to keep; that wasn't her fault. If she did find a job, someone there harassed her, or lied about her, or made life difficult; that wasn't her fault. Yes, she had friends who were using drugs, but she never used them; she was only trying to help her friends when they didn't have any other place to stay. When her so-called friends stole her food stamps and sold them for drugs, that wasn't her fault, either. These were the problems I could see but could not control or affect with my "advise." I knew their living conditions were not good, that they were barely existing on welfare and living in government subsidized housing. She had little money, but being poor was not the problem. Many good and honest people have grown up in poor households. I knew that all was not well, but there was nothing tangible I could see or identify. I never saw bruises or marks of any kind on the children, and they seemed to be happily living out their childhood with the kind of carefree abandon you would expect children to have. Emotional and sexual abuse carries no visible marks. Those kinds of abuses are well hidden from view, especially from the eyes of probing parents or grandparents. Hidden so well, because even the mother who is with the children every day cannot or does not want to see the abuse going on in her own home, abuse committed by so-called friends, hidden away in the dark places of night. Yet I could feel that something was not right. My questions, however, only brought protests of anger and resentment from my daughter, and my advice or offers of help were seen as accusatory and unwanted. To step in and take the children had certainly crossed my mind, but without tangible proof of wrong-doing or abuse, the courts would not back me, and I would only succeed in alienating my daughter. I did not want that.

The one thing I could do was pray. I believe that God hears our prayers and answers them, even if He does not always give us the answer we want. I prayed that God would watch over my grandchildren, and that He would help my daughter find the help she needed to raise them. He answered my prayer, by giving them to me.

I wish I did not have to raise my grandchildren, but I am glad I can. My husband Ben and I have been blessed with the financial means to provide them with the basics of life, as well as many of the extras. I have to balance being the frugal parent who must pay for the everyday needs of three growing girls, and being the grandmother who wants to spoil them rotten with every pleasure they want and I want for them. I love to see their eyes light up when we give them special gifts or surprise them with something they were not expecting. But I hate to be the one who has to dole out discipline when those gifts become the center of arguments between sisters, or have to take away a prized toy as punishment for failing to do homework or disobeying a rule.

I had expected to grow old gracefully, with children and grandchildren visiting on weekends, or enjoying long summer vacations together. My mind's eye saw pictures of happy family gatherings at holidays, birthdays, or for special outings. I imagined adult children who would dress up their children for a day at Granny and Pa-Pa's house; or, perhaps we would enjoy a day of picnicking at a park where we would chat about jobs and promotions, the children's latest adventures, or just enjoy each other's company. Instead, the only child of mine that had children of her own could not manage a life of her own. Happy family gatherings occurred at my house only if I drove there to pick them up and bring them to my house. Dressing up the children meant putting someone else's second-hand clothes on them, and there was never talk of jobs and promotions, only welfare checks and of how unfair the system could be. When my response was that if you do not like the system, then get out of it and get a job, I was met with the standard set of objections, or blamings, and cold, sullen faces because I "just did not understand." Family gatherings turned into gatherings of resentment and excuses. Most encounters left me feeling helpless, and robbed me of the ability to sleep for at least a night or two.

Life did not deliver what I expected; it seldom does. Instead of the happily-ever-after version I had hoped for for myself and my children, I received the life-goes-on version. But to refuse delivery is not an option. I accepted it, signed for it, and now I own it.

"Granny, come play basketball with me," Cindy begged.

I was already in my nightgown and housecoat when she wanted to play a summer evening game of basketball. "I can't play basketball in my slippers," I moaned.

"Yes, you can. You won't have to run. If the ball rolls away, I'll go get it," she promised.

I was glad we live in the country, in the middle of eleven acres of land, and that we do not have any neighbors close enough to see me shooting basketball in my housecoat and slippers. But at the same time I realized that within a few short years she would be the one who would not want to be seen by the neighbors, playing games with her grandmother, whether in a housecoat or fully dressed. We both laughed as I tossed the ball toward the hoop, missed, and watched her chase the ball and take her own shot. Of course, she scored higher than I did and declared it a fun game when she beat me. I am glad I decided to embrace that moment in her life. I tucked it away in that place were all

17

Hilda Osborne

precious memories are kept so that they can be pulled out and relived in years to come when such moments become the treasures of our lives.

CHAPTER THREE

Ask Me About My Grandchildren

Many grandparents proudly post bumper stickers that challenge the reader to "ask me about my grandchildren." The sentiments expressed on that bumper sticker have become my way of life. I tell everyone about my grandchildren, whether they have asked me or not, because I am still that oh-so-proud grandmother. Many times, I talk about my grandchildren by way of explanation. I explain that I cannot attend a particular event because I have to, or prefer to be at home with my granddaughters. A Saturday afternoon trip with the girls is much more inviting to me than the company picnic where the focus is a keg of beer. A church social where the girls' self-esteem and spiritual health is fed is more important to me than extra hours spent at the office. I join in conversations with young parents who discuss the perils and pleasures of parenthood, and am happy to be able to share my experiences with young people who seem to appreciate the sage advice and experience of a grandmother. Like any grandmother, I understand that all children are special, but none are as special as mine.

Cindy

As soon as she was legally old enough to do anything without my permission, my daughter exercised her new freedom by getting married. Less than three months after her 18th birthday, she called me one night and said, "Guess what I did today? I got married!"

She had married a boy, also 18-years-old, who had no education, no future, and no front teeth. He had a job in a used car lot, washing the cars and sweeping up the front office. But he had proclaimed his love for her, and all she wanted out of life was a man who would love her and take care of her. Even though he did not have much of a job then, and certainly no real ambitions in life, she was sure he would change if they were married. The trouble was, he was looking for the same thing in a partner that she was – someone who would take care of him. Ten months after their marriage, she gave birth to her first baby, a little girl she named Cindy.

About six months later, she was divorced.

When the girls came to live with us, ten-year-old Cindy was already accustomed to taking care of her little sisters. Because she was the oldest, she was often put in charge of watching them while her mother was busy doing something else. With the younger two in kindergarten and first grade, it was fourth-grader Cindy who would get them up and out the door for school while their mother slept. When Summer went to school one day during the winter without her coat, it was Cindy who flagged down a police officer to give them a ride home because her little sister was freezing. She was the one who boldly removed the piece of furniture blocking the kitchen door one Saturday morning so that she could get breakfast for the three of them, an act that cost her a whipping with a belt for disturbing her mother's husband, a whipping that she did not forget for a long time. "It's just not right," she would tell me, "to whip a little kid just for being hungry and trying to get some food."

That painful memory as well as many others haunted Cindy for a long time. If I needed to wake her in the middle of the night to give her medicine, or if I had to simply get something from her room while she slept, I would speak quickly and gently, "It's just me, Cindy." If she were startled from her sleep, I could almost hear the sound of her heart stop beating as she gasped and jumped. Even in a darkened room, I could see the fear on her face during that brief moment between waking and then realizing where she was and who was in the room with her.

When my husband and I went to bed in our room, we would close our bedroom door. One night Cindy asked me to leave it open. "What if something happens and you don't hear us?" she asked. I assured her nothing was going to happen to her or her sisters, but if it made her feel better, we would leave the door open.

Cindy struggled through the fifth grade. She had failed the fourth grade, but had gone through summer school to make it up. However, eight weeks of summer school cannot make up for a year's worth of bad grades. She was promoted to the fifth, but she had a hard time catching up to where she needed to be. Her grandfather and I did what we could to help her with her assignments, but not having dealt with school work for many years, and with having all but forgotten what we learned in school, many times we were just as lost as she was. That first year we were not only trying to adjust to having three more people living in the house with us, but also trying to get Cindy through the difficult fifth grade. We all managed to survive that first year, and Cindy was promoted to the sixth grade. She has become a good student, and now makes good grades on her own, with only a little help every now and then.

Cindy is now approaching 15, has just started as a freshman in high school, and is anxious to get her driver's learning permit. These days, it is the door to her room that stays closed. Even with the door closed, I hear can hear the thump-a thump-a of her music or the low whispers between her and friends late at night when they come for a sleep-over. She has rock-star posters on her walls, and a telephone to her ear for as many hours during the day as we will allow. She helps feed and groom the German Shepherd Dogs we raise, and goes roller-skating every chance she gets. She is everything a typical teenager should be, and those fears that once haunted her nights are a part of her past. She has not completely forgotten, however, and is planning a future as a lawyer. Someday she wants to be the one who puts bad people like the ones who abused her behind prison bars.

Lesley

Cindy was two years old when her mother realized she was pregnant again. She was not married to the baby's father because he was already married to someone else. Their relationship had been a casual one, and there was no love involved. This loveless, casual relationship would now produce a child who would not be claimed by her father, and who would inherit her mother's maiden name for her own.

I am not opposed to mixed relationships. Certainly, love comes in all colors. But such relationships can have their own special kinds of problems, and children that result from a mixed relationship have their own special needs. Two people of different color, culture, and background should be strongly united and prepared to deal with those unique situations before they plan a life together. And if that life includes children, they must be prepared to provide those children with the security of a strong home life where they can build the kind of strength and self-confidence that will let them move forward in their lives.

Identity is vital to children. They learn who they are by looking into their parents' faces, and the faces of the family that surrounds them to get an image of themselves. Lesley had no image of herself. Everyone close to her, her mother and both her sisters, had light skin, with blonde hair and blue eyes. Her skin was dark, her eyes a deep brown, and her hair was a mass of brown curls. No one looked like her.

She hated her hair. She dreamed of having long, blonde hair like her sisters. Lesley felt different from everyone around her. The only person she really felt connected to was her mother, and her mother was no longer in her life. There was little I could do to relieve the sadness I saw on her face day after day. When she talked of wanting long, straight hair, I pointed out that most people with straight hair were not happy with it, and wished for curly hair. But that did not make her feel much better.

"Granny," she asked me after getting off the school bus one afternoon, "am I Black?"

I was surprised by her question. "Yes, sweetheart, you are half Black. Your daddy was African-American. I thought you knew that."

"I do," she paused, then spoke with all the weightiness of a sad nine-year-old, "but all my friends think I'm White, and Summer keeps telling them I'm Black."

"You are half Black. But there is nothing wrong with that. Why would you want them to think you are only White? You should be proud of who you are." Summer could not have intended any malice toward her sister. To her, a fact is a fact, and the fact that her sister was half Black was simply that, a fact. For Lesley, though, it was just one more thing that made her stand out as different.

We have a beautiful view from the front of our house. We overlook a lake, and there are mountains on the other side, toward the west where the sun sets every day. As Lesley lay across her bed watching the sunset through the window one evening, I asked her, "That's a pretty sunset, isn't it?"

"Yeah," she answered still staring out the window.

"Did you know you will never see another one just like it?"

She turned to look at me and wrinkled her face to show that she did not understand what I meant.

"Every sunset is different. The sun is in a slightly different position everyday. Sometimes there are clouds in the sky, and sometimes there are no clouds. If there are clouds, they will be different from the day before. There may be a lot, or there may be a few. The clouds reflect the colors from the sun's rays and that is what makes the sky so pretty as the sun goes down. You will never see two sunsets that look exactly alike."

When she understood what I meant, I went on, "God can create many, many sunsets. No two are just alike, but they are all beautiful. God creates many kinds of people. We are not all alike, but we are all beautiful in His eyes." And I told her, "When you were born, do you think God said, 'Oops, I didn't mean to do that!'"

That got a giggle from her. "No," she said.

"Of course not. God knew who you were even before you were born, and He wanted you to be here." She needed to understand that she is an important person, a valuable creation of God. This was only the beginning of Lesley's long journey toward self-esteem and worthiness.

Although it was difficult for me to hear, I wanted Lesley and Cindy to feel comfortable talking to me about the terrible abuse they had suffered. Lesley needed to talk more often than Cindy. I would listen as she told me details of certain sex acts committed on her, the kind of sex acts that no child should have knowledge of, much less have experienced. I let them talk, and tried to answer their questions as honestly and as openly as I could. With each conversation, I assured them no one would ever do that to them again. One such conversation involved both Lesley and Cindy. We had closed the door to the bedroom so that we could have our "private talk" and the two of them sat cross-legged on the bed. As we talked, and the conversation finally reached a stopping point, the girls were beginning to squirm and roll around on the bed. In an instant, the talk went from a very adult theme to two little girls laying on their backs, hanging their heads off the side of the bed and giggling at an upside world.

Adjustment has not come easily for Lesley. She misses her mama more than the other two girls. She daydreamed of going back home to live with her mama for the first few years she lived with us. She has only recently started to accept the fact that she most likely will never live with her mama again, at least not as a child. She has had some counseling, and that helped. However, she was the one who told me when she had had enough visits to the counselor. "I just want to put all this behind me," she said in a very mature statement, "and at counseling I have to remember it every week."

She is starting to look toward her future. The first year she was here, she failed the second grade. Her grades have fluctuated with her moods from very good to very bad. As she enters the fifth grade this year, she is determined that she will be in the Beta Club. To be a member of the Beta Club, her grades cannot fall below a "B." We do not push the girls to make extremely high grades, and we tell them that a grade of "C" is acceptable as long as they are doing their best. On the other hand, we do not expect them to settle for "C" work. We let them know that we are very proud of them when they made grades above that. Also this year, Lesley was chosen to be a part of a trial program where students will learn to use technical equipment like computers and cameras. As a computer technician myself, I know there are wonderful possibilities for her in that field, if that field is what she ultimately chooses for herself.

Lesley has also become content with the person she is. She is no longer concerned with looking different from her sisters because she knows she does not have to look like them to be herself. Regular visits to a good hairdresser, along with learning how to manage her special curls, have helped her learn to like her own hair and to feel special in it. Just recently, she told me that now when her friends at school ask her how she got "mixed" she tells them, "They took a little of this, and a little of that, and they stirred it up real good, and they got me!"

Summer

While she was still pregnant with Lesley, my daughter met a young man whose introductory line to her was, "What would you do if I came over there and kissed you right now?" She called it love, and he soon moved in with her. He had no job and no money. The only things he contributed to the relationship were a cocaine habit, a violent temper, and a third baby. They named her Summer.

Summer was six years old when she came to live in our house, and although she apparently was not abused in the horrible ways her sisters were, she still carried issues that a six-year-old child should not have. She had seen too much adult behavior from the people her mother chose to let into her life, the kind of behavior that should have been hidden from the innocent eyes of a child. It was her first grade teacher who called me at home shortly after they were settled into their new school to tell me she had had to separate Summer from a little boy during story time. They were sitting too closely. They had arms wrapped around each other while holding hands at the same time. Later that summer, it was a Vacation Bible School teacher at a neighborhood church who apologized for being a snitch, but thought I should know that she had separated Summer and a little boy several times because they were holding hands during activity period. It took several stern talks before Summer began to accept the fact that she was entirely too young to even think about having a boyfriend.

For the most part, Summer has been everything you would expect of a normal little girl. She prefers getting dressed up in pretty dresses to wearing pants, and likes full skirts that stand straight out when she spins around. Summer has a wonderful out-going personality and manages to become the center of attention wherever she goes. She loves to twirl and dance, and as long as anyone's eyes are focused on her, she will happily entertain for as long as anyone will watch her. There are moments, however that she entertains not just by dancing or spinning but by some of the things she unwittingly says. We tease her that she is a "typical blonde" or we say we have experienced a "Summer moment" when she says something that is totally illogical or non-sense. One day her grandfather asked her to get a cardboard box that was sitting on a table in another room for him. "OK," she was eager to help. "What does it look like?"

Of course, we make sure she knows we are only teasing, and she gets to enjoy the fun as well.

School has been a struggle for Summer. She was in the first grade when she arrived here, and she had a difficult time even with the simple things a first grader should have been able to grasp. Second grade was even more difficult for her. At the end of the year, her teacher called me to say that even though her grades were low, she was borderline and just close enough that we could promote her to the next level if I chose to do so. Knowing how she had struggled throughout the school year, I felt it was in her best interest to let her repeat the second grade, and so that is what she did.

As a young parent who has an infinite number of years in front of them, one more year added to a child's school life may not seem like much. But as a grandparent whose years are not as plentiful as they once were, each year added is one more long year of raising a child. It means one more year of making sure lunch money is available, that there is an ample supply of notebook paper and pencils, that permission forms arc signed, and that she is ready for the bus each morning when it arrives at the end of the driveway. One more year added onto all the years already in front of us. But the effort we make is for her, for the child, so that she will have a chance at a better life, and we know her only chance is in a good education. One more year was a small sacrifice to help ensure she got it, right from the beginning.

During the summer months, the girls get to sleep in a little later than they do during the school year, sometimes sleeping as late as 10:00. For a special event, however, one morning we all rolled out of bed at 5:00am and started our road trip well before breakfast. By 8:00am, Summer was complaining that she was so hungry her stomach was hurting her.

"How can your stomach be hurting?" asked Pa-Pa. "When you sleep late and don't eat breakfast till 10:00 or 10:30, your stomach doesn't start hurting."

"But Pa-Pa," she explained, "when I sleep till 10 o'clock, my stomach sleeps till 10 o'clock, too."

CHAPTER FOUR

<u>Rules and Routines</u>

Going anywhere with three little girls when you are accustomed to going alone or only with other adults is a challenge. Whether for church, shopping, or just to a fast food restaurant, getting them bathed, dressed and their hair brushed could drive me to frustration and nervous tears, many times forcing me to give up and scream, "Forget it! We're not going!"

Hair preparation was a major event. Until the girls were old enough to manage their own hair, it was up to me to comb, brush, blow-dry, and/or coax four heads of hair, mine included, into something tame and fashionably acceptable. First mine, then the youngest, who required more of my attention than the other two. On one occasion when we were getting dressed for a social event at our church, I made sure the youngest was dressed, combed, and ready to go before I gave her strict instructions to sit down and be still until everyone else is ready to go. Next come the other two who, thankfully, prefer to play a major part in dressing themselves and styling their own hair. Finally, just on the verge of being late, we are all ready to leave the house. I look for the youngest who is no longer sitting where I told her to sit and stay. I find her instead in front of the bathroom mirror, before a sink full of water into which she is dipping a comb, and her sleeve, scooping up water and running it through her hair. "What are you doing?" my nerves yell at her.

"I'm fixing my hair," she appears surprised that I would even ask.

When we did manage to actually organize and go out into the world, chaos did not stop when we left the house. On arriving at our destination and attempting to get everyone out of the car in some sort of orderly fashion, it was not unusual to hear cries of, "Wait for me, I have to put my shoes back on," or "Granny, will you help me get my socks on; will you tie my shoes for me?" For the girls, being in a moving vehicle meant removing articles of clothing. In winter, even on the coldest days, coats and shoes automatically came off within the confines of the backseat.

"We always did it when we lived with Mama. She didn't care," became their defense. It took a while to teach them that one does not remove shoes and socks, or coats, or anything else when one is in a vehicle. "I forgot," or "Mama always let us" became a part of every arrival until they finally learned that arriving fully dressed at our destination was not optional.

Pulling into the parking lot of their favorite fast food restaurant, I knew to start issuing orders before the car stopped rolling. "Do *not* get out of this car until I tell you to!" Until I learned to get quick control of them, doors would fly open and the children would tumble out of the car before I had even turned off the motor. When we were stopped and parked, the next reminder came, "You can get out now, *but do not* walk across the parking lot until I tell you to." Too many close calls with cars driving through parking lots and children whose only thought was to be first inside and first in line made it necessary to keep tight reigns on them. Once inside, they had to learn to stand in line and wait to order their food. To them, the restaurant was another playground. They wanted to run from one table to another. Other patrons were assaulted with cries of, "Let's sit here; no, let's sit over there … You can sit there; I'm going to sit here … Granny, sit by me … No, it's my turn to sit by her, you sat beside her last time …" One of the girls might climb atop a table and announce, "Look how tall I am!" The youngest thought it was great fun to play hide and seek under the tables. After having to physically pull her out from under a table where other diners were eating one day, my husband swore his Taco Bell days were over!

In addition to restaurants, the grocery store was a wonderland for them. Everything was there for their taking. Just grab it, drop it into the shopping cart, and it was yours! The youngest enjoyed playing hide and seek in the grocery store, too, and would disappear behind displays or around corners. When she wasn't disappearing, she was sliding on her knees on the tile floor. She would get a running start, then drop to her knees throwing her arms up in the air the way she had seen ice skaters do on television. She would slide as far as she could on the shiny, buffed surface.

One shopping trip was especially difficult. I was down to my last nerve and they were wrecking havoc on it. The girls were full of energy and curiosity. Each one was going her own way, ignoring my instruction to stay with me or to stop grabbing things off the shelves.

"Oh, Granny, please get some of this, it's my favorite. Please, please, please, please!" one begged.

"Let's get some of this, — what is it?" It was wrapped in pretty colors. She did not know what it was, but she wanted it.

"Oh, look, we haven't had any of this for long time," cried another.

They played games of hide and seek, popping up from behind aisle displays to yell "Boo!" They ran their hands across everything on every shelf within reach. If we were not going to buy it, they were at least going to touch it. They walked slowly in front of the shopping cart when I wanted to walk fast, or held the side of it as they walked along, blocking the aisle for other shoppers and making it difficult to navigate through the crowded store. I listened to cries of "get this," "get that," and issued orders to deaf ears until I could take no more.

"If you don't walk quietly behind me, you are all going to go sit in the car until I'm finished, and I will never bring you to the store with me again!" A few minutes later, realizing compliance with my edict had been too complete, I turned around to see impish grins and hear silly giggles from three little girls marching in a straight line directly behind me, walking when I walked and standing at perfect attention when I stopped. What a sight that must have been for the other shoppers!

Laundry duty more than tripled. Three little girls can produce more dirty clothes in two days than my husband and I could produce in a week, or at least it seemed that way. I washed, sorted, and folded baskets full of clothes, leaving them on beds with instructions to put them in drawers or hang them, as neatly as they could, in the closet. When I began finding the same clean clothing, still folded, in the dirty laundry basket a week later, I decided it was time for them all to learn how a washing machine operates. Each was provided her own laundry basket, and each one received personalized instructions on how to put dirty clothes in the washer to wash, to move them to the dryer to dry, and to place the clean clothing in the proper drawers. Even as the oldest nears her mid-teen years, they are still perfecting the art of laundry, but as long as they emerge from their rooms wearing clean clothing, I do not let myself worry (too much) about the condition of their closets and drawers.

In the beginning, mealtime was so hectic it almost drove us to give up eating. The girls had been accustomed to fending for themselves and had never been taught any table manners. Mealtime was "grab what you want before somebody else gets it" time. Seats had to be assigned to avoid arguments over who would sit where. Meal time brought excited shouts of "What are we having? ... I don't want any of that! ... I want lots of this. ... Where's mine? ... Don't take it all!"

The children had to learn to sit down and be patient. No one is going to go away hungry, I assured them. There was plenty for everyone and everyone will get a plateful. They also had to learn how to stay seated at the table. At any moment during the meal, any one of them might jump up to get something off the counter or race around to the other side of the table to grab something she wanted. Or maybe it was something unrelated to the meal. One would suddenly remember a toy – a doll she felt she should "feed" – and would make a mad dash to the bedroom, sometimes with a second child in hot pursuit to make sure "she doesn't get my doll." Remembering a song could bring singing and dancing, bouncing and spillage to the table. Mealtime rules had to be made and implemented quickly:

1. Sit down at your appointed place at the table.
2. Wait for your plate to be served.
3. Wait for your drink to be placed beside your plate.
4. Wait for a spoon or fork to be given to you.
5. If you need something from the counter or the other side of the table, ask for it.
6. No singing or dancing at the table.
7. No getting up from the table without permission.
8. The only reason to ask permission to leave the table before a meal is finished is to go to the bathroom.

    a. Wash your hands after you go to the bathroom.

9. Go to the bathroom before you come to the table.

    a. Wash your hands after you go to the bathroom.

10. If you leave the table without permission, 1 will assume you are finished and will take up your plate.

One night, after telling Summer to get dressed for bed, I walked into the bedroom she shared with her sister. Lesley had made the unusual choice to go to bed early that night, and was already sound asleep. I expected to find Summer ready to be tucked in and waiting for her good-night hug. Instead, I found her engrossed in painting her sleeping sister's face with colored lip gloss.

Life had become anything but routine.

CHAPTER FIVE

Discipline

Discipline is not a word grandparents like to associate with their grandchildren. A grandparent's reward in life is to enjoy the children of their children. To discipline or punish a child for doing childish things only produces long faces and tears of disappointment – from the grandparents. Spoiling the children (within reason, of course) and enjoying their company before sending them home with their parents offers a special kind of satisfaction and reward for all the long years of raising our own children. We feel we have left our marks on the world in the form of perfect little lives that will grow into perfectly successful adults. But when the grandparents who spoil the children must become the parents who deal with them on a daily basis and who take on the responsibility for teaching and disciplining, everything changes.

Before the girls came to live with us, our life was quiet and simple. With just my husband, myself and the German Shepherd Dogs we raise, we never had to deal with situations that called for planned discipline. Other than the occasional sternly spoken "no" and snap of a leash, followed by "good dog" and a pat on the head, we did not have to think much about discipline. Now, however, we had to learn to bring order out of chaos for three little girls who had never been taught how to be orderly. They had to learn about discipline, and not only the kind of discipline that comes as a result of some bad behavior. Discipline is also the art of conducting life in an orderly and acceptable fashion.

There must be hundreds of books written on the proper ways to discipline children, and few of them agree. Attitudes and opinions range from the old fashioned school of thought that to spare the rod is to spoil the child, to the notion that you can reason with a child, and that if he or she understands why a certain behavior is bad, he or she will refrain from exhibiting that bad behavior. It is my opinion that those people who believe you can reason with children have never raised children.

Spanking is a controversial subject, and there are a variety of arguments for and against it. It has never been my assertion that spanking should be avoided altogether. In certain situations, spanking has its place. These girls, however, had already experienced the wrong kind of spanking, the kind that was only meant to control and frighten, not to correct or teach. But I still needed to emphasis the fact that bad behavior brings about unpleasant and undesirable results. I wanted to do everything I could to avoid spanking, so that meant coming up with some creative methods of discipline.

Disciplinc should be a balance of teaching and nurturing, as well as a demonstration that bad actions result in unpleasant consequences. Depending on the nature of the infraction, the consequence could be losing a favorite toy (which the grandmother side of me wants to give back when she sees even the slightest bit of repentance and improvement), to being grounded to their rooms or standing with face turned toward the wall for a prescribed length of time.

We live in a rural area where getting to school means riding the school bus. The bus route begins at the farthest point from the school, then works it way in. We live at that farthest point, so the girls are among the first to be picked up in the mornings and the last to be dropped off in the afternoons. They spend a lot of time on the school bus. Misbehaving on the bus simply cannot and will not be tolerated. The bus driver must deal with 20 to 30 children in a confined space and, at the same time, be aware of traffic or road hazards which in our area could mean a cow in the road or a deer darting across from a nearby field. The girls had to learn that a bus is not a playground. During their first year of being picked up and dropped off by the bus, it was not unusual to see long faces as we were handed notes from the bus driver. They would not stay in their seat. One had hung her head and arms out the bus window, performing her favorite songs to an imaginary audience. Another experimented with sitting upside down, putting her head where her feet should be while propping her feet where she should have put her head. Tossing balls, making loud noises, screaming, yelling, and being generally unruly produced notes and warnings of being suspended from riding the bus for a three-day period. Although we talked, we lectured, and we grounded, eventually the note came that said two were suspended and would not be allowed to ride the bus to school for three days. They still had to be at school, which meant we had to drive them there and pick them up again. Driving them to school did create something of an inconvenience, and I was angry that the girls would not obey simple safety rules on a moving bus to the point that they were not allowed to ride that bus for a while. The bus drove past our house as I loaded the errant girls into the car to drive them the eight miles to school before I continued on my way to work. But to drop them off at the front door of the school seemed to be a reward for bad behavior, and I became the one experiencing the punishment, not them. I decided they would not enjoy a free ride to the front door of the school building. Instead of driving them all the way, I dropped them off one-half mile from the school. This is a reasonable walking distance. I dropped them off, but stayed with them to make sure they made it to school safely. I watched them walk ahead several yards, then pulled the car up and past them. I parked at the curb and watched as they approached and passed me. I continued this "leap-frog" game until I saw them enter the school door. I felt this made a stronger impression on them that riding the bus is a privilege that should not be taken lightly. After three days of making the half-mile walk up hill, while carrying a backpack full of books and homework, they began to appreciate that privilege.

Household furnishings that have sat quietly serving their individual purposes for years were suddenly victims of abuse. Window blinds became twisted and torn, and pull-stops were suddenly missing from the ends of the pull-cords. Curtains were tugged on until the rods were pulled out of the wall. The children had to learn that towel bars were meant to hold only towels, and not little girls who wanted to hang from them. An antique bed suddenly and mysteriously developed deep carvings on one of its bedposts. Sharp-edged rocks were discovered just below small cuts in the window screens, and plaintive little voices were heard saying, "I just wanted to see what it would do."

The girls were not accustomed to following rules. No one had ever bothered to explain rules to them, or that certain behavior is expected in certain places, or why. Bedtime was never a specific time that was set so that they would get the proper amount of sleep that a growing child needs. They stayed up as late as their mother stayed up. This was her way of ensuring they would not wake her too early in the morning. If one of the adults in their life was angry, they might get a smack, or someone might lash out with a belt. They were punished if someone saw them as an annoyance. Otherwise, they were pretty much on their own, to do whatever they liked, as long as they did not get in the way of any of the adults in their lives.

I confess there have been times when I have experienced "good child envy." I see other parents gently instructing their little ones, and these well-behaved children respond by doing exactly as they are told. They are polite and walk unobtrusively through shopping malls, or sit quietly on benches or in movie theaters. Not like my girls. For them every new situation or public place equals the pure, unbridled excitement of discovery. Strangers are just friends they haven't annoyed yet. Gumball machines are something to shake until a free prize falls out. Restaurants become playgrounds, and parking lots turn into racetracks where the fastest gets to stand in line first. At home, they have to be reminded to wash their hands after going to the restroom; in public restrooms, they want to wash, rinse, and wash again, jabbing at soap dispensers and squishing foam through their fingers until they are wilted. And it did not take them long to discover that the hand blowers feel wonderful on your hands, on your head and down the front of your shirt!

Discipline is not easy. I'd rather be spoiling them. But discipline and rules are a must in all walks of life, and to not teach them proper behavior is not fair to them nor to the people they will encounter on various levels in their lives. The schoolroom demands that they know how to sit still and pay attention. Playgrounds demand that they know how to play nicely and to share equipment or toys with other children. Public places require that they show consideration for other people who occupy the same space or participate in the same activity, whether it is watching a movie, eating a meal, or picnicking and swimming at public parks. Real discipline, the kind that is handed out in love and with explanation, was not something they had had in their lives. Teaching them to behave according to a set of rules was like trying to take sudden control a bunch of baby chicks. They all want to go in several different directions at one time, and you can never predict where they will end up. Nothing had ever been required of them, and to teach them now that they had to do certain things within certain guidelines presented new challenges and were met with responses like "but we always did it like that" or "Mama always let us."

We, like most grandparents, must reach for energy that is not as abundant as it once was, and must use that energy to correct and discipline a child because someone else failed to teach that child. Most children who come to live with their grandparents are not coming from homes where they were taught or nurtured in the way children should be taught. As a result, they bring with them many bad behaviors, and it is up to those grandparents to change these bad behaviors. For some, including parents and grandparents as well, it may appear to be easier to ignore bad behavior, allowing the child to grow up with bad habits that can be destructive later in life. It takes time, energy and determination to be attentive to a child's behavior and to help that child grow into a responsible adult in our society.

We do keep reaching, however, and we keep finding the energy we need because we understand the importance of proper teaching. We discipline, we teach, and we make sacrifices. We demonstrate that discipline is not just a word that means punishment; it also means participating in life in an orderly and accetable manner. We also go to ballgames, attend school conferences, school plays, and science museums. We dig through schoolbooks to find the right answer, and we gather everything that is needed to create special projects for extra credit at school. We save our energy by cutting out some of the things we would have done in order to bring life to the things they want to do, and to teach them discipline so that they can do those things successfully.

Bedtime for the girls is something Ben and I look forward to, even if they do not. It is those few moments at the end of the day when they are finally settled in bed that we can begin to settle our minds or have a conversation without interruptions.

At bedtime one Friday night, Lesley wanted to stay up past her appointed time. "We don't have to go to school tomorrow. Why can't we stay up?"

"Your bedtime has nothing to do with school," I teased. "It is for my mental health."

Hilda Osborne

CHAPTER SIX

That's Entertainment?

In the beginning, there was rock 'n roll. At least, that is what it was called in the days of my youth. It had a beat, and you could dance to it. The most scandalous thing about our music was the way Elvis moved his hips while insisting that we stay off his blue suede shoes. The Beatles appeared on the scene with their unimaginably long, shaggy hair enticing otherwise neatly-cut young men to follow suit, and driving respectable young girls to scream uncontrollably, cry and declare their undying love right there in public, with camera rolling. Our music was different from that of our parents, just as our music is different from that of our children. And just like our parents, we are sure those mesmerizing notes that were surely devised by the devil himself are leading our children down a path of mayhem and self-destruction.

While our generation was not destroyed by the music we listened to and neither was the generation that followed us, I must say I have great concerns about the steady diet of suggestive lyrics streaming into my grandchildren's ears.

"Granny, cut it up! That's my favorite!" No matter how loud the radio is when one of their favorite songs comes on, one of them is sure to cry out, "Cut it up! Cut it up!" They are never amused when I made scissor-like cutting motions with my fingers toward the radio knob. "Granny, hurry. I want to hear it!" I was wasting precious time and the song would surely be over before I could get it loud enough to be heard in the back seat.

Airbag safety concerns prevented any of them from sitting in the front seat next to me for the first couple of years they were with us, so the music I enjoyed came from the back seat. Music to my ears was the laughter and chatter of three little girls enjoying the beat from the radio or from their own voices and imaginations. Before then, I had never paid much attention to the latest pop hits and had no idea of who the current teen idols were. I was blissfully unaware of sex-encrusted lyrics and bare midriffs punctuated with bellybuttons that had been punctured for the sole purpose of inserting decorative items of jewelry. The girls were not so unaware, but could sing along with most of the songs, and knew far too many of the disturbing lyrics.

"Hit me, Baby, one more time..." It was the only part of the song that caught my attention and made me sit up and listen. The girls had come from a situation where boyfriends and husbands took liberties to hit the women they claimed to love. And, sadly, the women around them allowed the abuse on themselves, simply by not making changes or eliminating those men from their lives. No man has a right to hit a woman, and no woman should ever tolerate such abuse. The lyrics of the song they were repeating over and over seemed to be reinforcing the idea that somehow women wanted to be "hit" by the men who were supposed to love them. I was not going to support this idea that "hit me" and "baby" could be used together in the same sentence.

"But, Granny, you don't understand," they insisted.

I watched the video that portrayed an attractive young girl in an all-too-short school uniform skirt as she moved in suggestive gyrations in what appeared to be a school hallway lined with student lockers, pleading with someone to hit her one more time. Oh, I understood all right. My grandchildren were forbidden to sing those words, and I refused to purchase any material produced by that particular artist.

Sex sells; it always has and it always will. In our dollar-driven society where everyone wants to top the music charts or beat their competitors by selling more of anything, whether it is music, the latest fashion, or floor wax, sex is the sales gimmick of choice. I was not convinced that a young girl in a school uniform which, by the way, was much shorter than any respectable school would ever allow, moving suggestively down a school hallway was not intended to stir the animal lust that drives so many people straight to the music and video stores to purchase the thing that was presented to them disguised as a young girl's innocence.

Some may argue that a song is only a song. A few words set to music with a good beat.

But when fed into the minds of children and young teenagers, the lyrics of a song become more than just words. They become the images of what they think the world outside their world is like. If the images are damaging, vicious, or overtly sexual, children accept them as normal. If the images present unattainable beauty and perfection, children begin to believe they must be just as beautiful and perfect. When they fail to attain that perfection, they feel they have failed and loose any sense of self-worth. They do not realize that many of the stars they admire attain their "natural beauty" through expensive professional trainers, plastic surgeons, and serious food deprivation.

And it is not just the images on the stage or on videotape than can influence young lives. Every teenager who can read a teen magazine holds the very lives of the popular TV and music stars in close scrutiny. Reports of where they go and who they go with are followed closely by teenagers who talk about their daily activities as if they were next-door neighbors. While riding with my oldest granddaughter one day, I listened as she excitedly chattered on and on about her friends at school, their favorite pop stars, and her favorite songs. I was only half listening as she told me more than I really cared to hear about what was going on in this star's life or another singer's life. She was talking about a popular female artist who reportedly was slapped by her boyfriend. The rumor was she said something he did not like, and he slapped her.

She said, "Heather said she probably deserved it."

"Hold it right there." She now had my full attention, and I wanted to make sure I had her attention as well. "No woman ever deserves to be slapped. Nothing a woman can do gives any man the right to hit her." I have serious doubts that the story of the singing star being slapped by her singing-star boyfriend was true, but Hollywood rumor control was not on my agenda for today. My only concern was that my granddaughter fully understand that no woman ever deserves to be slapped. I repeated my words to her, "There is *NOTHING*," I emphasized, "that a woman can do to deserve being slapped."

"I know that," she said. But I was not convinced she really *knew* that.

"Did you tell your friend Heather that?"

"Umm.., no."

"Tell her. The next time you see her, you tell her that your Granny said, 'No woman ever deserves to be hit.'"

Too many young girls think a slap or a hit from "their man" is normal. Too many women accept this vicious act as a natural part of life. To allow someone to say "I love you" one minute, then cause bodily harm or pain the next minute is not acceptable. Nor is it acceptable to see it perpetuated by any song or rumored life-style.

Ben and I enjoy movies in our leisure time. We thought nothing of picking up a rental that we wanted to see. Adult scenes were all right because, well, we are adults. Now we think carefully before allowing movies that the girls might see. I have become keenly aware of situations that might create the kind of image I do not want growing in my grandchildren's minds. We have learned we cannot depend solely on how the movie is rated. Even some PG-13 movies have contained material that we considered inappropriate for a 13-year-old.

Recently, we were convinced to rent a popular movie that "all their friends" had been allowed to see. Their grandfather and I sat down to watch it before we would allow them to see it. Only about ten minutes into the movie, we did not want to see any more of its crude sexual humor, much less allow our granddaughters to see it. When we returned it to the video store the next day, the man behind the counter understood. "I did not care for it," he said. "Too much emphasis on genitalia."

There was a time when comedians made you laugh by finding the funny side of everyday life. We laughed at men and women who were willing to act silly in front of an audience. There are a rare few comedians who still do that, but most prefer to appeal to the base side of human nature and make "genitalia" their main focus. Make jokes about the human body and you are an instant success. Too many times the producers of so-called comedy want to treat their audiences as if the only thing they will laugh at is sexual dysfunction or absurdities that are better left behind closed doors.

While there are many movies that we will not allow the girls to see, having a family movie night is still one of their favorite things to do. We will select a good movie that we think everyone will enjoy. We pop popcorn or have pizza. The focus is not the movie itself, but the fact that we are together, being entertained together, as a family. It is important to give the girls a sense of family, and entertainment, the right kind of entertainment, plays a major part in that.

The girls can watch the same movie over and over again, and enjoy it even more than they did the first time they saw it. On one trip to a video rental store, Lesley picked out a movie that they had all seen a dozen times already. I picked out another for myself.

"Have you seen that one before?" Lesley asked me.

"No, I have never seen this one," I told her.

With a puzzled look she asked me, "But Granny, if you've never seen it, how do you know you'll like it?"

CHAPTER SEVEN

Gum On The Floor

"Why is there gum on the floor?" I call out, or more accurately, yell out. I get the expected response – silence. If I do get any answer at all, I hear, "Not me." Of course it was *not me*. *Not me* seems to be the culprit behind most of the mischief in this house!

I do not really need someone to tell me why gum is stuck to the floor; I already know. There is gum on the floor because there are children in the house. Certain conditions exist in our universe that are inseparable. If you have one of these conditions, you must have the other. Gum on the floor, something sticky on the refrigerator door, handprints and streaks of dirt on the walls are a few of the unchangeable conditions of having children present. Creative little minds leaving behind

71

tiny clippings of paper all over the floor, crayons to be stepped on and mashed into the carpet, and elusive glitter that teasingly sparkles at you out of the corner of your eye. Missing toys, misplaced hairbrushes, and cries of "that's mine, leave it alone!" are all a part of the natural order of things in a household that contains children.

My husband and I are adjusting to this new order of things. We had grown accustomed to the fact, for example, that if we put something on a table or in a closet, it would still be there when we returned for it. However with children in the house such expectations are too often met with the grim fact that nothing is guaranteed to still be at that same location where it was once seen or left. Ink pens are especially notorious for growing legs and walking away. Like stray puppies, they can spot a child from a mile away and will follow that child's every move until she reaches out and makes it her own. And no thoughtful little girl would leave a single sheet of clean paper to feel neglected or unwanted. That is why every sheet of paper in the house has some kind of scribble or mark on it. It may be a spiral that starts in the middle of the page and grows and grows until it fills up the whole page. Or it could be a single, mis-spelled word or scribbled mark in the upper margins, leaving the rest of the page abandoned because "I messed it up."

At one time my supply of bath and makeup items, along with my few pieces of jewelry were safe from hands other than my own. But with three little girls in the house, *my* bath powders, *my* shampoo and conditioner, *my* gold necklace, and anything else I could rightfully call *mine* has become a part of the public domain known as *ours*.

"But you let me use it the last time," becomes the reasoning I hear when I realize little fingers have been into something for which I did not give permission this time. And you can be sure that the same child who thinks she has been granted permanent access to her grandmother's personal supplies will be the first one to scream at her sister, "I said you could use my crayons yesterday. I didn't say you could color with them today!"

Toothpaste tubes are squeezed from the middle, and caps are left off by the mischievous "*not me*" who used it last. Band-aids become badges of honor that cover mosquito bites or imagined injuries, leaving none available when there is a real need to cover a bleeding wound. Superglue is accidentally "spilled" on the carpet, and items lost in plain site are all a part of the universe that spins around the household that contains children.

At one point I thought I had to control all of these events in order to maintain order in our home. Instead, I was creating just the opposite. Trying to maintain the "place for everything, and everything in its place" mentality and enforcing that rule requires more energy than I have to give at this point in my life. I have learned that if it is not going to matter in five years, or in five days, it does not matter now. Gum can be scrapped up and cleaned away in much less time than it takes to discover the culprit who managed to let gum fall unnoticed out of her mouth and onto the floor. Walls can be cleaned with a quick spray and a wipe. In fact, this is a task the youngest child loves to perform. Give her a bottle of 409 spray, a cleaning cloth, and turn her loose. She can entertain herself for hours. Granted, it may not be as good a cleaning job as I would do, but most of the dirt gets obliterated, and I will give it a good cleaning the next time, and there will be a next time, the mysterious *not me* runs her dirty hands along the hallway wall or splatters a drink across the floor.

"*Why did you leave your doll on the kitchen counter?*" *I asked her.*

"*So I would remember to take it to my room later.*"

"*So you laid the toy on the counter, so you could take it to your room later. But then you went to your room?*"

"*Yes.*"

"*Why didn't you just take the doll with you as you went to your room?*"

"*I don't know.*"

CHAPTER EIGHT

A Special Name

Lesley is the only one of the three who does not have a clear picture in her mind of her biological father. Cindy had something of a relationship with her daddy up until she was six years old. And Summer's daddy was in and out of their lives for several years before his cocaine habit finally carried him to the outer fringes of reality, where, as far as we know, he is still clinging. But Lesley's daddy was a part of her mother's life only long enough to produce a child. He was long gone before she was borne. The other two children have the last names of their fathers; Lesley has her mother's maiden name. She has never had a daddy she could identify with, no face to picture, no sound of spoken words to remember. For her, there was no daddy. This was not something she could accept. For a child, having no real daddy, or at least one she can picture in her mind, is devastating. It becomes a part of her identity, or lack thereof.

"Pa-pa," she asked Ben one day, "can I call you Daddy?" She had recently started calling him "Pa", a shorten version of the name the girls use for their grandfather, but also a name used by the children she had seen in some old westerns for their daddy. He was the first one to relate his sudden change in title to her need to relate to a father figure.

"Of course you can," he told her. "You can call me Daddy, or Pa, or Pa-pa, whatever you want."

She was thrilled to have someone she could call *Daddy*. That night, during our ritual of good-night hugs and kisses, as she hugged her grandfather, she said, "Good-night, Daddy." Then, with a big grin, "I've always wanted to say that."

Her sisters were surprised when they heard her call him "Daddy." Summer, the youngest, gave her a puzzled look, and asked, "Why are you calling him *Daddy*?"

"Because he is my Daddy now."

A bright smile lit up Summer's face. "Can I call you *Daddy*, too?"

"If you want to," he told her.

"OK, good-night, *Daddy*," she giggled.

Cindy, who stays up a little later because she is a little older, asked him after the other two had left the room, "How did you get to be her *Daddy*?"

Cindy knew and missed her daddy. Despite the fact that he had not been a real parent, and that he had made no attempt to even stay in touch with her, she missed him. It made no difference to her that he had left the state and would not hold a job for fear of being forced to pay child support. For her, no one could take her daddy's place.

"Lesley needed someone to call *Daddy*," I tried to explain. "You can call him *Daddy*, too, if you want to."

"Well," she said in the most apologetic voice she could manage for a thirteen-year-old, "I love you and all, Pa-pa, but *daddy* is kind of a special word."

"Exactly!" I realized that she had pin-pointed the issue so much better than I could have. "And Lesley has never had anyone she could apply that special word to. You have memories of your daddy, you know his name and what he looks like, Lesley doesn't. And even Summer can at least identify her daddy and call him by name. Lesley has no memory of a name or a face that she can put in that place where a daddy should be. There is a big hole her life and she needed someone to put in that empty space.

"But it is all right if you do not want to call Pa-pa *Daddy*," I did not want her to think we expected it from her, or that her grandfather might be hurt if she did not. "This is just something Lesley needs."

Pa-pa continued to be *Daddy* for a while. But when Lesley decided she would rather call him Pa-pa, because that is what he was to her, we told her we understood. But we left the option open, so that she knew she could call out to *Daddy* anytime she wanted, and someone would respond to her.

While "daddy" may be one of the most important words in their vocabulary, the thought of "their daddies" can conjure up ugly words and thoughts in my mind. "Daddy" does not always represent what is good and right in a child's life. In the case of my three granddaughters, there was not one good daddy in the bunch.

I like to think I have reached a point in my life where my values and well thought-out bits of advice are gifts I can offer to the younger generation. I have lived many years, and I have paid attention to what works and what does not work. I like to think that my patience and understanding of the greater picture of life, and of the whole system by which all of humanity functions and the world turns makes me the one to come to for answers to the perplexing questions and for examples of how to behave in a particular situation. Not always so.

As the girls were having dinner one evening, the subject of their daddies came up. My husband had prepared the meal they were eating, right down to shopping for the groceries, thawing out the meat, and buttering the vegetables. He had cooked it on the stove, spooned it out onto plates and set it in front of them. I came in late from work that evening and, as usual after a day in a call center listening to other people complain about their problems, I felt drained. There was still homework to help with, and baths to be orchestrated. The kitchen would have to be cleaned tonight, or someone would have to deal with the mess tomorrow. I still had hours of work in front of me. As I was preparing my plate to sit down at the table with them, the girls were arguing over who had the best daddy.

"Well, at least I met my daddy. You don't even know who your daddy is," the oldest never missed an opportunity to antagonize either of her younger sisters.

"I have, too, met him," Lesley was defensive. "Don't you remember when Mama woke me up in the middle of the night one time. She told me 'you want to see your daddy, don't you?' and I got up and I saw him."

The girls had different daddies, and they had all been through some bad experiences because none of the fathers were willing to take on the responsibilities of raising a child. I bit my tongue many times to avoid saying bad things about the men who gave them biological life. I did not want to criticize them or put them down, at least not in front of the children. After all, they were still their daddies, and every child should at least enjoy the fantasy of a daddy who loves them. When anything concerning their biological fathers came up, I would steer them away from the negative thoughts, and would make every attempt to enforce the idea, at least to the girls, that their daddies did love them, each in their own way.

This one evening, however, I was tired. They argued about who had the best daddy, and whose daddy cared more than the other one. One was happily recalling that her mother had awakened her in the middle of the night to "see her daddy." I could not control my anger when Cindy asked me, "Granny, who has the best daddy?"

"None of you do," I snapped. "Which one of your daddies stood at this stove, cooking your supper tonight? Which of your daddies even cares if you're eating anything tonight? Which daddy is here every morning, making sure you have breakfast or that you get off to school on time? Which daddy gives you lunch money every week or buys you shoes and clothes, or pencil and paper when you need them? Which daddy is here in the middle of the night when you are coughing or you are sick, and which daddy takes you to the doctor and makes sure you get the medicine you need? Your Pa-pa is the one who does that, and he's the best daddy any of you have!"

Well, so much for all that carefully thought-out wisdom and patience.

Several years ago, the image of the "super-mom" slipped into our lives. She was the mother who could do the unnatural – maintain a full-time job, keep the house sparkling clean, and be there for whatever her husband and children needed. We have subsequently learned there is no such thing as a "super-mom," but what about "super-grandparents?" So many of us are asked to start all over, raising children we ourselves did not plan nor give birth to. We are older, our patience is thinner and our tolerance for irresponsibility is low. We took care of our responsibilities, why can't everyone else take care of theirs. We bear the burden of what others, younger and stronger, simply walk away from. It is a difficult assignment, an assignment that does not leave us with amiable feelings toward the one or ones who put us in this position. And that one, in most cases, is called "Daddy."

Ben had just brought home a new DVD player. After we finished watching a movie on it, he asked Summer to take the disk out of the disk tray. She was amazed when the tray opened automatically when she got close to the player.

"How did it do that?" she asked in amazement.

"Wave your hand over it," Ben told her. When she did, the tray magically closed again.

Over and over, she waved her hand in front of the DVD player and was mystified every time the drawer opened or closed.

"Lesley," she called to her sister when she walked into the room. "Watch what I can do!"

Lesley watched the drawer slide open as Summer moved her hand in front of it, but she caught on quickly.

"Uh-uh," she pointed out. "I see Pa-Pa pushing that button!"

He laughed as he held up the remote control to demonstrate the source of her "magic."

Hilda Osborne

CHAPTER NINE

Ticklebelly Hill

There is a spot on the road that leads to our house that rises about ten feet and then makes a small but sudden drop just as you get to the top of the small rise. To me, it was just another bump on our road. The road follows alongside a wide creek, and the pavement rises and falls much like the rushing water just a few feet away. The road makes its way between the creek on one side and a steep hillside on the other that was cut away to make this country lane. There are many dips and rises in the road, but one in particular was pointed out by a friend of one of the girls. I had picked her up at her house to bring her to our house to spend the night with Cindy.

"Speed up, speed up!" Nicole called out as we got closer to the small rise in the road that was so familiar to me.

"Yeah, Granny, speed up!" My granddaughter chided in excitedly. She already knew the secret. If you speed up just a little as you go over the rise, the small but sudden drop on the other side is just enough to create a falling sensation in your stomach. You won't find it marked on any maps and there are no signs along the way to indicate it, but all the kids in this area know this spot as Ticklebelly Hill. I pressed the gas pedal just enough to built up a little speed. We bounced just slightly as we went up and over the little rise, and felt the little tickle in our bellies. The girls all laughed and squealed as if they had just ridden their favorite roller-coaster.

That is it, I thought. That is what childhood should be. Children laughing at tickling sensations and happy moments filled with delightful little surprises. The happy surprises, the friendships, and all the fun experiences that go into making a childhood were what I wanted for my grandchildren. Abuse, fear, worry, and doubt are words that should never enter into a child's world. Bumps in the road should mean tickles in the belly, not problems or conflicts. Life's journey should have us passing over those little spots that make us want to squeal with laughter, and children should spend their time building happy memories.

Now when I make that drive down our road, I press the gas pedal, cautiously of course, just a little harder as I approach the spot known as Ticklebelly Hill. The car accelerates as it reaches the top of this little mound, then drops, producing the desired tickle. I am delighted to hear their laughter and squeals of joy as the girls bounce and get that tickle in their belly. I can no longer drive down our road, and probably never will, without remembering this special spot and the simple joy it invokes. Whether or not the girls are with me, I still enjoy that little tickle.

It is the memories of the happy times with our children that we will treasure the longest. The difficult times will fade away, but the happy moments will be reinforced and will become brighter each time we recall them. I know, because I have been down this road before. I traveled this road while raising my own two children. I have forgotten many of the twists and turns, and have purposely put out of my mind those places in my journey whose memories only sadden me. But I hold tight to the treasures, the laughter and the happy moments that I tucked away in my heart while my children were growing up. I now do the same thing with my grandchildren.

Sometimes I feel saddened as I gather the treasures that rightfully should be gathered by my daughter. She does not know what she is missing. Her children will one day grow into adults, and she will never again have the opportunity to see them as the children they are now. Her life has been hard, mainly because of choices she made, and she cannot see anything beyond that hard life. For her, raising children was just one more hardship she was not able to deal with. There is no doubt that she loves them, and I would not have them think otherwise. The girls are in close touch with their mother, for which I am grateful. That would not be possible if the girls were in a state-supervised foster care system. But while she sees the girls frequently, and is kept up-to-date on their school progress and daily activities, one day she will experience an emptiness, a loss of something she did not even know she had.

Hopefully, one day she will be able to reach out to her own grandchildren. She will give them gifts of toys, pretty clothes, and out-stretched arms. If she is fortunate, she will enjoy picnics in the park with her family, and conversations about jobs, promotions, and new friends. Her children will bring their children to her house, where she will spoil them rotten before sending them home with their parents.

We drove past an older model car that was sitting on the side of the road. The paint was a faded gray, there were numerous dents and dings all over the body of the vehicle, and the hood was raised. Its owner had obviously left it behind to go for help. On the back window were the words "For Sale, $200." Cindy, who is approaching the age of getting her driver's license and wants a car of her own said, "Granny, you could buy that car for me and I could fix it up. I could get someone to fix the motor for me, and I could get it painted, and it would be as good as new."

"Now you sound just like your mother," I answered her. I had seen too much money disappear when she would try to fix up old things, money that would have been better spent on newer, working models instead of something that could be bought cheap and fixed up. "She was always saying the same kind of thing," I said.

Summer had been listening to the conversation and she was amazed. "How long has that car been sitting there?" She asked.

Appendix

According to the AARP Foundation, over 4.5 million children under the age of 18 are living in households headed by a grandparent. (http://www.aarp.org) Of these households, over 2 million do not include either of the child's parents. The reasons for this vary, but include the death of one or both parents; parents who are unable to care for their children because of drugs, illness, or poverty; or because of abuse the children have suffered.

Grandparents who are raising their grandchildren deal with mixed emotions. They suffer feelings of anxiety at being cast into the role of primary parent at a time in their life when they thought such responsibilities were behind them. At the same time, they want to care for their grandchildren to ensure they are nurtured in a safe and loving home. For these grandparents, it is a job they did not ask for nor did they expect to be doing at this time in their lives, but for them there is no other option.

If you are among the grandparents who are playing the role of parent to your children's children, you are not alone. There is some help, both emotional and financial, for grandparents who have taken on the responsibility of raising their grandchildren. Many church groups are beginning to see the need in their communities for programs that will reach out to these grandparents-turned-parents. Check with your local church or religious organization to find support groups in your area. Plus there may be some financial help available for low-income households. Contact your local Social Services office for more information.

There are several organizations where grandparents can find help and encouragement. Click, call, or write to:

The AARP Foundation
www.aarp.org/grandparents
601 E St., NW
Washington, DC 20049
Phone: (800) 424-3410

Grandsplace – A place on the internet for grandparents
www.grandsplace.com

Generations United
www.gu.org/projg&o.htm
Phone: (202) 638-1263

Join a **Ring of Grandparents** on the Internet by including your own website, or just be encouraged by browsing through the sites already in the ring:

www.fortunecity.com/millennium/castleton/11 23/rogp

The organizations and websites mentioned here are offered for information only. This is not an endorsement of their services nor is any guarantee made that the services will still be available at the time of publication or anytime thereafter. The author is not responsible for any actions of the sites or organizations named herein.

Hilda Osborne

About the Author

Hilda Osborne grew up in Nashville, Tennessee. She earned a Bachelor of Science Degree in Applied Organizational Management from Tusculum College by studying nights and weekends. English Composition 101 is where her talent for writing was first recognized. After she submitted a writing assignment, the instructor wrote at the top of the page, "Where did you learn to write? This is really good!" She currently resides in Roane County, Tennessee where she moved with her husband in 1987. Between the two of them, they have three children and five grandchildren (and counting).

913322

Made in the USA